40 Christmas Fav
for five finger patter

MW00748807

arranged by Richard Bradley

Bradley
Publications
a division of
RBR Communications, Inc.

Come they told me,
Parum pum pum pum,
Our new born King to see,
Parum pum pum pum,
Our finest gifts we bring,
Parum pum pum pum,
To lay before the King,
Parum pum pum pum,
Rum pum pum pum,
Rum pum pum pum.

So to honor Him,
Parum pum pum pum,
When we come.

The Little Drummer Boy

Words and Music by KATHERINE DAVIS,
HENRY ONORATI and HARRY SIMEONE
Arranged by Richard Bradley

The Little Drummer Boy - 2 - 1

Baby Jesu,
Parum pum pum pum,
I am a poor boy too,
Parum pum pum pum,
I have no gift to bring,
Parum pum pum pum,
That's fit to give our King,
Parum pum pum pum,
Rum pum pum pum,
Rum pum pum pum.

Shall I play for you,
Parum pum pum pum,
On my drum?

Mary nodded,
Parum pum pum pum,
The Ox and Lamb kept time,
Parum pum pum pum,

I played my drum for Him,
Parum pum pum pum,
I played my best for Him,
Parum pum pum pum,
Rum pum pum pum,
Rum pum pum pum
Then He smiled at me,
Parum pum pum pum,
Me and my drum.

4

Silent night, Holy night, all is calm, all is bright,
'Round yon Virgin Mother and Child,
Holy Infant so tender and mild.
Sleep in heavenly peace. Sleep in heavenly peace.

Silent Night

Words by
JOSEPH MOHR

Music by
FRANZ GRUBER

Arranged by Richard Bradley

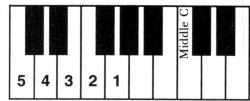

✻ Left Hand

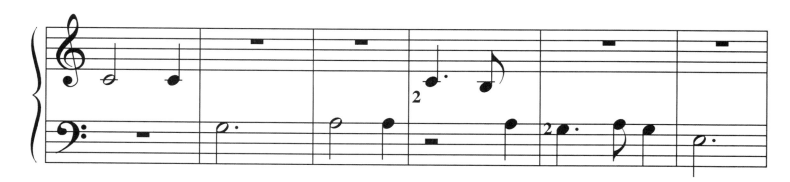

Change to second hand position

Silent Night - 1 - 1

Away in a manger,
No crib for His bed,
The little Lord Jesus
Laid down his sweet head.
The stars in the sky
Looked down where he lay.
The little Lord Jesus,
Asleep in the hay.

Away In A Manger

By JAMES R. MURRAY
Arranged by Richard Bradley

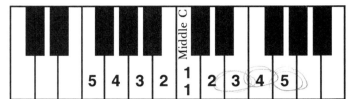

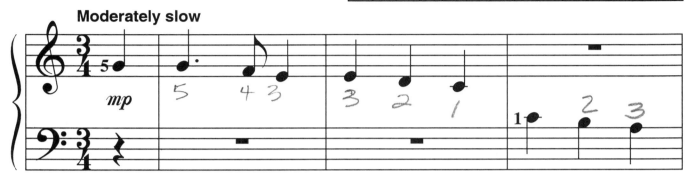

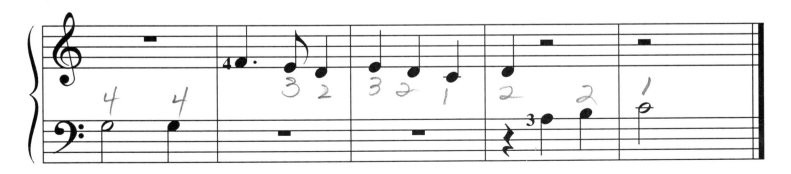

Away In A Manger - 1 - 1

Deck The Halls

TRADITIONAL
Arranged by Richard Bradley

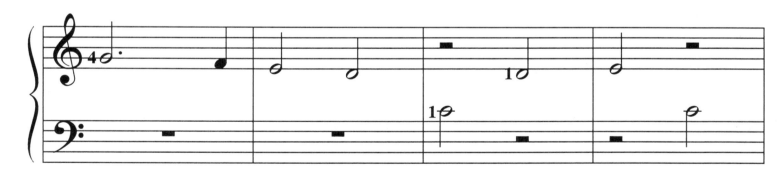

Deck The Halls - 2 - 1

Deck the halls with boughs of holly,
Fa la la la la la la la la!
'Tis the season to be jolly,
Fa la la la la la la la la!
Don we now our gay apparel,
Fa la la la la la la la la!
Troll the ancient Yultide carol,
Fa la la la la la la la la!

Let It Snow! Let It Snow! Let It Snow!

Words by
SAMMY CAHN

Music by
JULE STYNE

Arranged by Richard Bradley

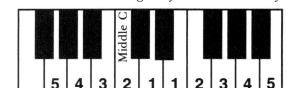

Oh! the weather outside is frightful,
But the fire is so delightful,
And since we've no place to go;
Let it snow! Let it snow! Let it snow!

It doesn't show signs of stopping,
And I brought some corn for popping;
The lights are turned way down low,
Let it snow! Let it snow! Let it snow!

Cheerfully

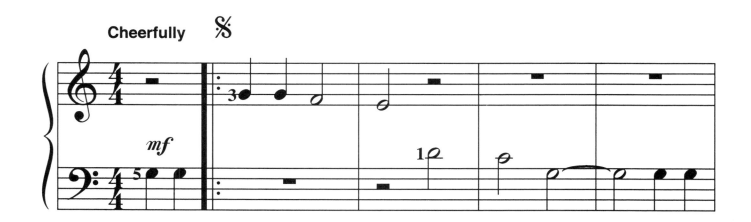

Let It Snow! Let It Snow! Let It Snow - 2 - 1

When we finally kiss good night,
How I'll hate going out in the storm!
But if you'll really hold me tight,
All the way home I'll be warm.

The fire is slowly dying,
And my dear, we're still goodbyeing,
But as long as you love me so,
Let it snow! Let it snow! Let it snow!

10

What Child is this who laid to rest,
On Mary's lap is sleeping?
Whom angels greet with anthem sweet,
While shepherds, watch are keeping?
This, this is Christ the King,
Whom shepherds guard and angels sing.
Haste, haste to bring Him laud,
The Babe, the Son of Mary.

What Child Is This?

By WILLIAM CHATTERTON DIX
Arranged by Richard Bradley

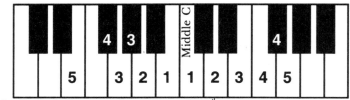

Left 3rd finger plays G and G♯
Right 4th finger plays F and F♯

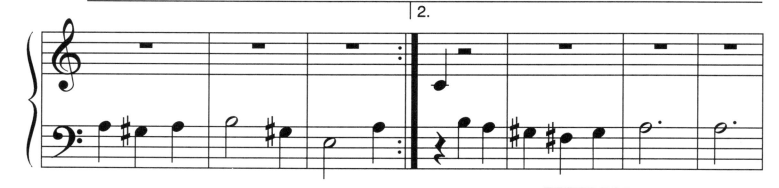

What Child Is This? - 1 - 1

The first Noel, the angels did say,
Was to certain good shepherds
In fields where they lay;
In fields where they lay
Keeping their sheep,
On a cold winter's night
That was so deep.
Noel, noel, noel, noel,
Born is the King of Israel.

The First Noel

TRADITIONAL
Arranged by Richard Bradley

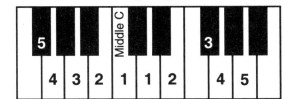

Moderately slow

The First Noel - 1 - 1

We Three Kings Of Orient Are

By J. H. HOPKINS
Arranged by Richard Bradley

We Three Kings Of Orient Are - 2 - 1

© 1994 BRADLEY PUBLICATIONS
All Rights Assigned to and Controlled by BEAM ME UP MUSIC (ASCAP),
c/o WARNER BROS. PUBLICATIONS U.S. INC., 15800 N.W. 48th Avenue, Miami, FL 33014

We three kings of Orient are;
Bearing gifts we traverse afar,
Field and fountain,
Moor and mountain,
Following yonder star.
O, star of wonder,
Star of night,
Star of royal beauty bright.
Westward leading,
Still proceeding,
Guide us to thy perfect light.

We Three Kings Of Orient Are - 2 - 2

All I want for Christmas
Is my two front teeth,
My two front teeth,
See my two front teeth!
Gee, if I could only have
My two front teeth,
Then I could wish you
"Merry Christmas!"

All I Want For Christmas Is My Two Front Teeth

Words and Muisic by
DON GARDNER

Arranged by Richard Bradley

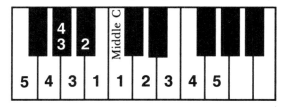

Left hand fingers 3 and 4 also play G♯

Moderately

All I Want For Christmas Is My Two Front Teeth - 3 - 1

It seems so long since I could say,
"Sister Susie sitting on a thistle!"
Gosh, oh gee, how happy I'd be
If I could only whistle.

All I want for Christmas
Is my two front teeth,
My two front teeth,
See my two front teeth!
Gee, if I could only have
My two front teeth,
Then I could wish you
"Merry Christmas!"

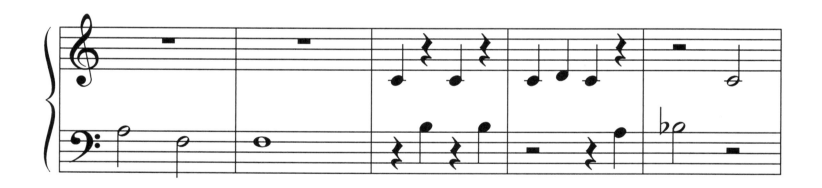

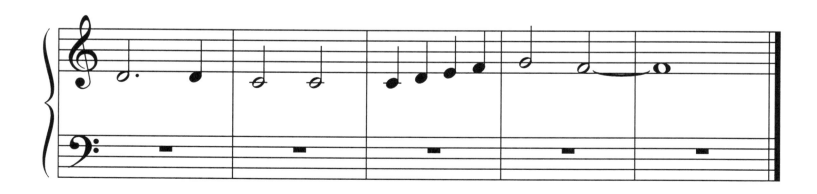

All I Want For Christmas Is My Two Front Teeth - 3 - 3

O come, little children,
O come, one and all.
O come to the manger
In Bethlehem's stall,
And see the Lord Jesus
Asleep in the hay.
The little Lord Jesus
Was born Christmas day.

O Come, Little Children

TRADITIONAL
Arranged by Richard Bradley

Moderately

O Come, Little Children - 1 - 1

Toyland! Toyland!
Beautiful girl and boy land,
While you dwell within it
You are ever happy then.
Childhood's joyland,
Mystic merry toyland!
Once you pass its boarders
You can never return again.

Toyland

Words by
GLEN MacDONOUGH

Music by
VICTOR HERBERT
Arranged by Richard Bradley

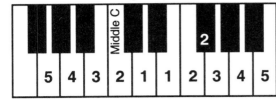

Right 2nd finger plays F and F♯

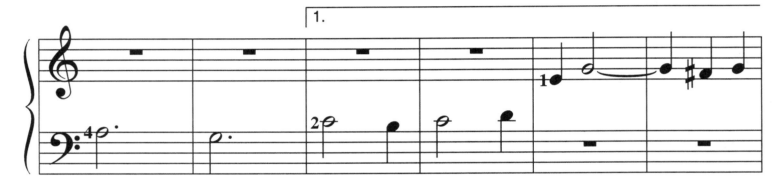

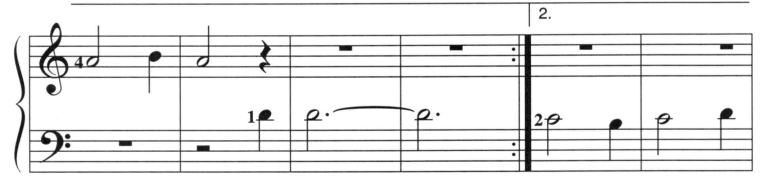

Toyland - 1 - 1

Angels we have heard on high
Sweetly singing o'er the plains.
And the mountains in reply
Echoing their joyous strains.
Gloria in excelsis deo,
Gloria in excelsis deo.

Angels We Have Heard On High

TRADITIONAL
Arranged by Richard Bradley

Angels We Have Heard On High - 1 - 1

Oh, there's no place like home for the holidays,
'Cause no matter how far away you roam,
When you pine for the sunshine of a friendly gaze,
For the holidays you can't beat home, sweet home.
I met a man who lives in Tennessee
And he was headin' for
Pennsylvania and some homemade pumpkin pie.
From Pennsylvania folks are travlin'
Down to Dixie's sunny shore.
From Atlantic to Pacific,
Gee, the traffic is terrific.
Oh, there's no place like home for the holidays,
'Cause no matter how far away you roam,
If you want to be happy in a million ways,
For the holidays you can't beat home, sweet home.

(There's No Place Like)
Home For The Holidays

Words by
AL STILLMN

Muisic by
ROBERT ALLEN

Arranged by Richard Bradley

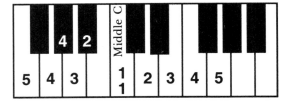

Left hand 4th finger plays G and G♯

Home For The Holidays - 2 - 1

Fine

D.S. ℅ al Fine

O come, all ye faithful,
Joyful and triumphant,
O come ye,
O come ye to Bethlehem.
Come and behold Him
Born the King of angels.
O come, let us adore Him,
O come, let us adore Him,
O come, let us adore Him,
Christ, the Lord.

O Come, All Ye Faithful

TRADITIONAL
Arranged by Richard Bradley

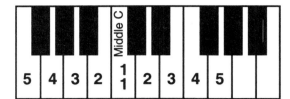

Majestic

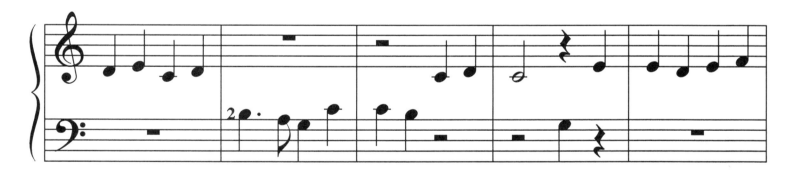

O Come, All Ye Faithful - 1 - 1

God rest ye merry, gentlemen,
Let nothing you dismay,
Remember Christ our Saviour
Was born on Christmas day,
To save us all from Satan's pow'r
When we were gone astray;
O tidings of comfort and joy,
O tidings of comfort and joy.

God Rest Ye Merry, Gentlemen

TRADITIONAL
Arranged by Richard Bradley

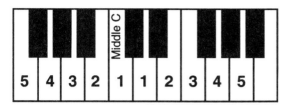

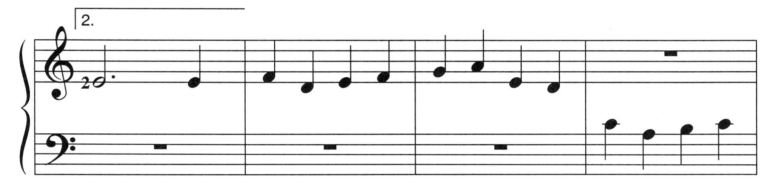

God Rest Ye Merry, Gentlemen - 1 - 1

It Came Upon A Midnight Clear

By EDWARD HAMILTON SEARS
and RICHARD STORRS WILLIS

Arranged by Richard Bradley

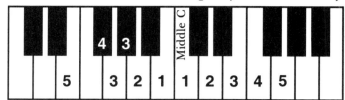

Left 3rd finger plays G and G♯

It Came Upon A Midnight Clear - 2 - 1

It came upon a midnight clear,
That glorious song of old,
From angels bending near the earth,
To touch their harps of gold.
"Peace on the earth,
Good will to men,
From heaven's all gracious King."
The world in solemn stillness lay
To hear the angels sing.

It Came Upon A Midnight Clear - 2 - 2

Sleigh bells ring, Are you list'nin'?
In the lane, snow is glist'nin',
A beautiful sight, we're happy tonight,
Walkin' in a winter wonderland!
Gone away is the bluebird.
Here to stay is a new bird.
He sings a love song as we go along,
Walkin' in a winter wonderland!

Winter Wonderland

Words by **DICK SMITH**   Muisic by **FELIX BERNARD**

Arranged by Richard Bradley

Left 3rd finger plays C and C♯
Right 2nd finger plays G and G♯

Play brightly

Winter Wonderland - 2 - 1

In the meadow we can build a snowman,
Then pretend that he is Parson Brown.
He'll say, "Are you married?" We'll say, "No man!
But you can do the job when you're in town!"
Later on, we'll conspire,
As we dream by the fire,
To face unafraid the plans that we made,
Walkin' in a winter wonderland.

Sleigh bells ring, Are you list'nin'?
In the lane, snow is glist'nin',
A beautiful sight, we're happy tonight,
Walkin' in a winter wonderland!

Gone away is the bluebird.
Here to stay is a new bird.
He's singing a song as we go along,
Walkin' in a winter wonderland!

In the meadow we can build a snowman,
And pretend that he's a circus clown.
We'll have lots of fun with Mister Snowman,
Until the other kiddies knock 'im down!
When it snows ain't it thrillin',
Tho' your nose gets a chillin'?
We'll frolic and play the Eskimo's way,
Walkin' in a winter wonderland!

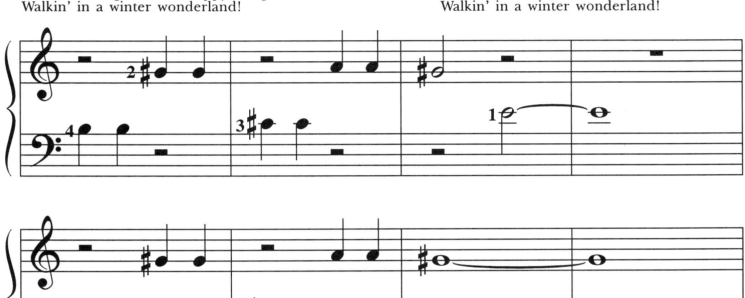

Winter Wonderland - 2 - 2

Dashing through the snow,
In a one horse open sleigh;
O'er the fields we go,
Laughing all the way.
Bells on bobtail ring,
Making spirits bright.
What fun it is to ride and sing
A sleighing song tonight!

Jingle Bells

Words and Music by
J. PIERPONT

Arranged by Richard Bradley

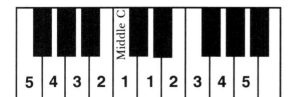

Jingle Bells - 2 - 1

Jingle bells, jingle bells,
Jingle all the way!
Oh, what fun it is to ride
In a one horse open sleigh!
Jingle bells, jingle bells,
Jingle all the way!
Oh, what fun it is to ride
In a one horse open sleigh!

Jingle Bells - 2 - 2

Christmas, Christmas time is near,
Time for joy and time for cheer.
We've been good, but we can't last.
Hurry Christmas, hurry fast.

Want a plane that loops the loop.
Me, I want a hula hoop.
We can hardly stand the wait.
Please Christmas, don't be late.

The Chipmunk Song
(Christmas, Don't Be Late)

By ROSS BAGDASARIAN, SR.
Arranged by Richard Bradley

Moderately bright

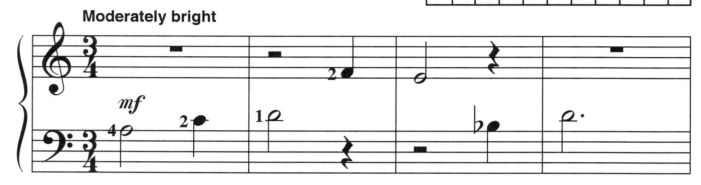

The Chipmunk Song - 2 - 1

Spoken:

Alvin: *Dave, I've been asking for that hula hoop for years.*
I would like to ask for something new, like roller skates
or a new stereo, but I have to have that hula hoop first.
Please Dave! I've been very patient.
Dave: *Alvin, just finish the song. We'll talk about it later.*

Want a plane that loops the loop.
I still want a hula hoop.
We can hardly stand the wait.
Please Christmas, don't be late.

The Chipmunk Song - 2 - 2

It's the most wonderful time of the year.
With kids jingle belling,
And ev'ry one telling you,
"Be of good cheer,"
It's the most wonderful time of the year.

It's the hap-happiest season of all.
With those holiday greetings,
And gay happy meetings
When friends some to call,
It's the hap-happiest season of all.

It's The Most Wonderful Time Of The Year

Words and Music by
EDDIE POLA and GEORGE WYLE
Arranged by Richard Bradley

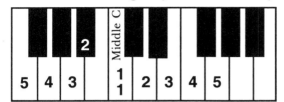

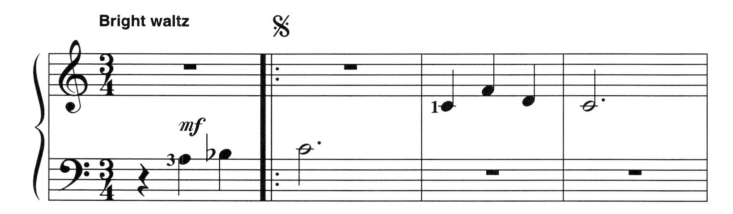

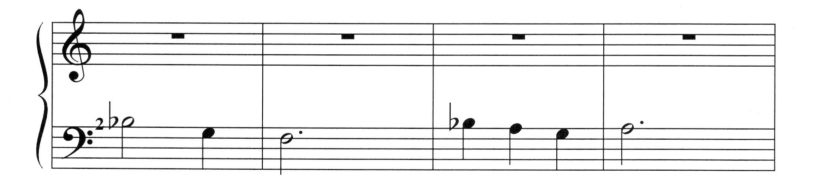

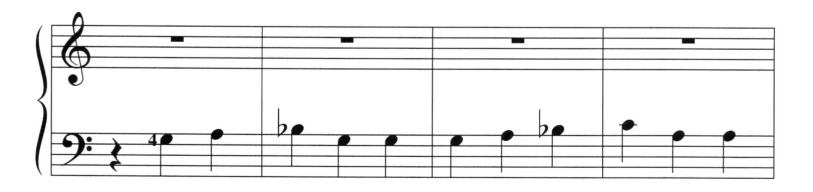

It's The Most Wonderful Time Of The Year - 3 - 1

There'll be parties for hosting,
Marshmallows for toasting
And caroling out in the snow.
There'll be scary ghost stories
And tales of the glories
Of Christmases long, long ago.

It's the most wonderful time of the year.
There'll be much mistletoeing,
And hearts will be glowing
When loved ones are near.
It's the most wonderful time of the year.

It's The Most Wonderful Time Of The Year - 3 - 2

34

❋ Second position

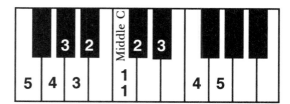

Left 3rd finger plays A and A♭

❋ Change to 2nd hand position

D.S. 𝄋 al Fine

It's The Most Wonderful Time Of The Year - 3 - 3

Jolly old Saint Nicholas,
Lean your ear this way!
Don't you tell a single soul
What I'm going to say.
Christmas Eve is coming soon;
Now you dear old man,
Whisper what you'll bring to me.
Tell me if you can.

Jolly Old Saint Nicholas

TRADITIONAL
Arranged by Richard Bradley

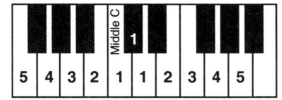

Left thumb plays C and C♯

Jolly Old Saint Nicholas - 1 - 1

O Christmas tree, O Christmas tree!
Thou tree most fair and lovely!
O Christmas tree, O Christmas tree!
Thou tree most fair and lovely!
The sight of thee at Christmas tide
Spreads hope and gladness far and wide.
O Christmas tree, O Christmas tree!
Thou tree most fair and lovely!

O Christmas Tree

TRADITIONAL
Arranged by Richard Bradley

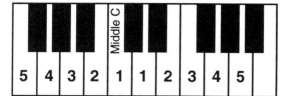

O Christmas Tree - 1 - 1

I wonder as I wander,
Out under the sky,
How Jesus, the Saviour,
Did come for to die,
For poor or'ny people
Like you and like I.
I wonder as I wander,
Out under the sky.

I Wonder As I Wander

TRADITIONAL
Arranged by Richard Bradley

Moderately slow

I Wonder As I Wander - 1 - 1

Have Yourself A Merry Little Christmas

Words and Music by
HUGH MARTIN and RALPH BLAINE
Arranged by Richard Bradley

Have yourself a merry little Christmas,
Let your heart be light,
From now on, our troubles will be out of sight.
Have yourself a merry little Christmas,
Make the yuletide gay,
From now on, our troubles will be miles away.

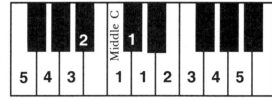

Left thumb plays C and C♯

Moderately slow

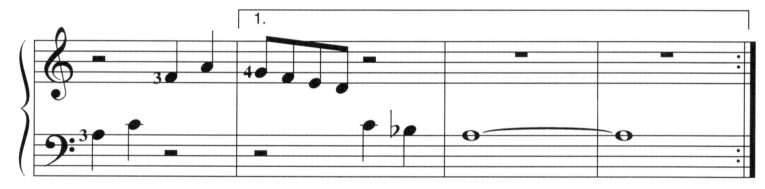

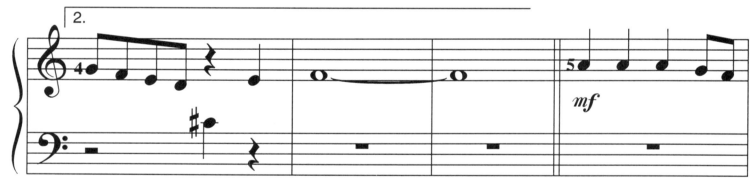

Have Yourself A Merry Little Christmas - 2 - 1

Here we are as in olden days,
Happy golden days of yore,
Faithful friends who are dear to us
Gather near to us once more.
Through the years we all will be together,
If the Fates allow,
Hang a shining star on the highest bough
And have yourself a merry little Christmas now.

❊ Right Hand

❊ Change to second hand position

First
❊ position

Have Yourself A Merry Little Christmas - 2 - 1

I'll Be Home For Christmas

Lyric by
KIM GANNON

Music by
WALTER KENT

Arranged by Richard Bradley

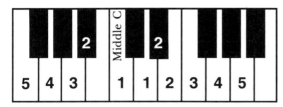

Right 2nd finger plays E and E♭

Moderately slow

I'll Be Home For Christmas - 2 - 1

I'll be home for Christmas.
You can count on me.
Please have snow and mistletoe
And presents on the tree.
Christmas Eve will find me
Where the love light gleams.
I'll be home for Christmas,
If only in my dreams.

I'll Be Home For Christmas - 2 - 2

O come, O come Emmanuel
And ransom captive Israel,
That mourns in lonely exile here,
Until the Son of God appear.
Rejoice! Rejoice!
Emmanuel shall come to thee,
O Israel.

O Come, O Come Emmanuel

TRADITIONAL
Arranged by Richard Bradley

O Come, O Come Emmanuel - 1 - 1

Hark! The Herald Angels Sing

CHARLES WESLEY
FELIX MENDELSSOHN
Arranged by Richard Bradley

Hark! The herald angels sing,
"Glory to the new born King!
Peace on earth and mercy mild,
God and sinners reconciled."
Joyful all ye nations rise,
Join the triumph of the skies.
With angelic host proclaim,
"Christ is born in Bethlehem."
Hark! The herald angels sing,
"Glory to the new born King!"

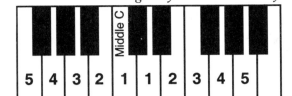

Majestically

Hark! The Herald Angels Sing - 1 - 1

You better watch out,
You better not cry,
Better not pout,
I'm telling you why:
Santa Claus is comin' to town.

He's making a list
And checking it twice,
Gonna find out who's naughty and nice,
Santa Claus is comin' to town.

Santa Claus Is Comin' To Town

Words by
HAVEN GILLESPIE

Music by
J. FRED COOTS

Arranged by Richard Bradley

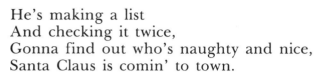

Right thumb plays C and C♯

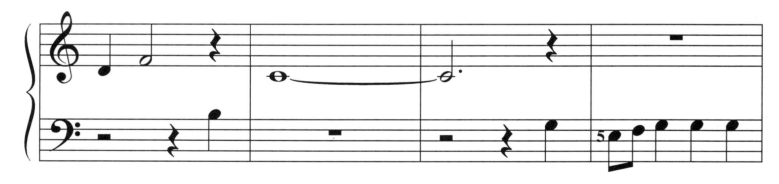

Santa Claus Is Comin' To Town - 2 - 1

He sees you when you're sleepin'
He knows when you're awake,
He knows if you've been bad or good,
So be good for goodness sake.

Oh! You better watch out,
You better not cry,
Better not pout,
I'm telling you why:
Santa Claus is comin' to town.

Santa Claus Is Comin' To Town - 2 - 2

Joy to the world,
The Lord has come!
Let earth receive her King!
Let ev'ry heart prepare Him room,
And heav'n and nature sing,
And heav'n and nature sing,
And heav'n,
And heav'n and nature sing!

Joy To The World

By ISAAC WATTS
GEORGE FREDERIC HANDEL
Arranged by Richard Bradley

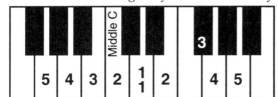

Majestic

Good King Wenceslas
Looked out on the feast of Stephen,
When the snow lay 'round about,
Deep and crisp and even.
Brightly shone the moon that night,
Though the frost was cruel
When a poor man came in sight
Gath'ring winter fuel.

Good King Wenceslas

TRADITIONAL
Arranged by Richard Bradley

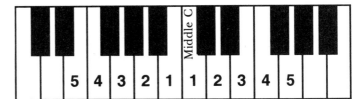

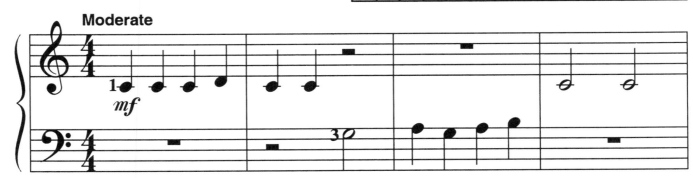

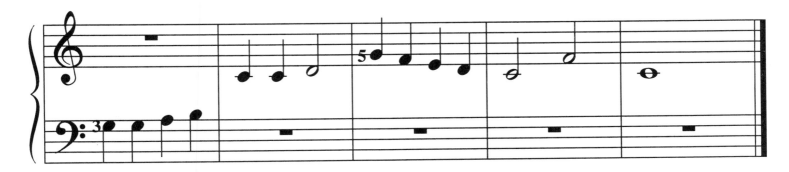

Good King Wenceslas - 1 - 1

I saw three ships come sailing in
On Christmas Day, on Christmas Day.
I saw three ships come sailing in
On Christmas Day in the morning.

I Saw Three Ships

TRADITIONAL
Arranged by Richard Bradley

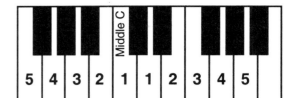

I Saw Three Ships - 1 - 1

O little town of Bethlehem,
How sweet we see thee lie,
Above the deep and dreamless sleep,
The silent stars go by.
Yet in thy dark street shineth,
The everlasting light;
The hopes and fears of all the years
Are met in thee tonight.

O Little Town Of Bethlehem

TRADITIONAL
Arranged by Richard Bradley

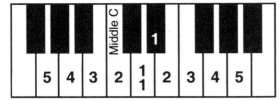

Right thumb plays D and D♯

O Little Town Of Bethlehem - 1 - 1

Frosted window panes, candles gleaming inside,
Painted candy canes on the tree;
Santa's on his way,
He's filled his sleigh with things for you and for me.
It's that time of the year when the world falls in love.
Ev'ry song you hear seems to say: "Merry Christmas,
May your New Year dreams come true."
And this song of mine, in three quarter time,
Wishes you and yours the same thing too.

The Christmas Waltz

Words by
SAMMY CAHN

Music by
JULE STYNE

Arranged by Richard Bradley

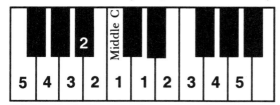

Right 2nd finger plays B and B♭

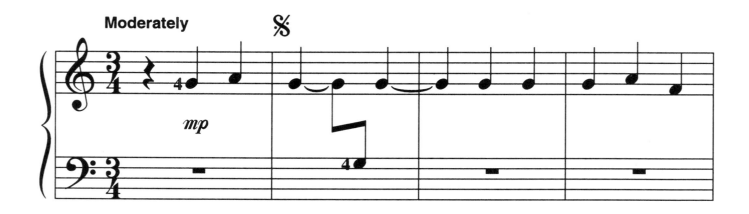

The Christmas Waltz - 2 - 1

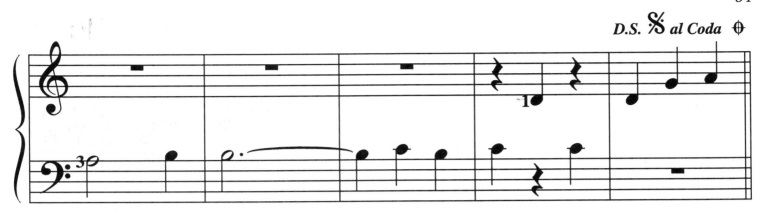

Coda
⊕

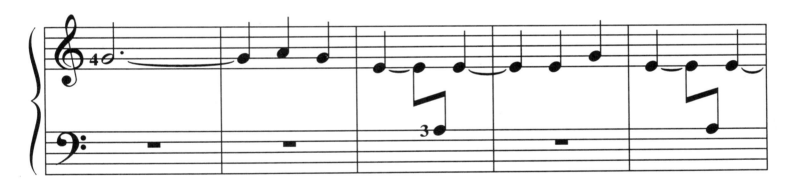

We Wish You A Merry Christmas

TRADITIONAL
Arranged by Richard Bradley

We wish you a merry Christmas,
We wish you a merry Christmas,
We wish you a merry Christmas,
And a happy new year!
Good tidings to you,
Wherever you are;
Good tidings for Christmas
And a happy new year!

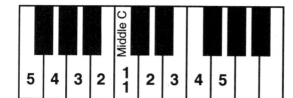

Cheerfully

We Wish You A Merry Christmas - 1 - 1

Pat-A-Pan

TRADITIONAL
Arranged by Richard Bradley

Willie, take your little drum.
Robin, bring your fife and come.
When we play the fife and drum,
Tu-re-lu-re-lu, pat-a-pat-a-pan.
When we hear the fife and drum,
Christmas should be frolicsome.

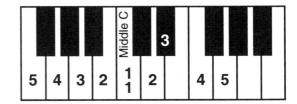

Pat-A-Pan - 1 - 1

O holy night!
The stars are brightly shining.
It is the night of the dear Savior's birth.
Long lay the world in sin and error pining
Till He appeared and the soul felt its worth.
A thrill of hope, the weary world rejoices
For yonder breaks a new and glorious morn.

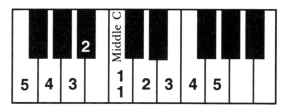

O Holy Night

Words and Muisic by
ADOLPHE ADAM

Arranged by Richard Bradley

Moderately slow

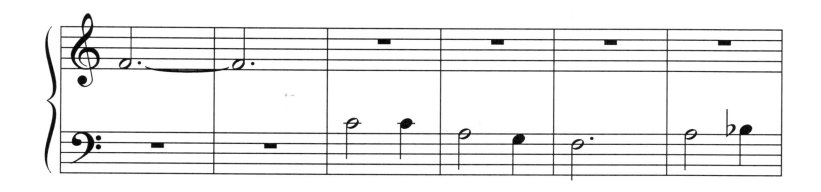

O Holy Night - 4 - 1

Fall on your knees!
O, hear the angels voices!
O night divine.
O night when Christ was born.
O night divine!
O night, O night divine.

O Holy Night - 4 - 2

Right Hand F Hand Position

Original Hand Position

When I was a learner,
I sought both night and day.
I asked the Lord to aid me
And He showed me the way.

Go tell it on the mountain,
Over the hills and ev'rywhere.
Go tell it on the mountain,
Our Jesus Christ is born.

Go Tell It On The Mountain

TRADITIONAL SPIRITUAL
Arranged by Richard Bradley

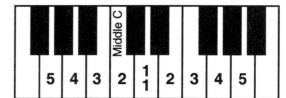

Go Tell It On The Mountain - 1 - 1

Up on the housetop reindeer pause,
Out jumps good old Santa Claus.
Down through the chimney with lots of toys,
All for the little ones Christmas joys.
Ho, ho, ho; who wouldn't go!
Ho, ho, ho; who wouldn't go!
Up on the housetop; click, click, click.
Down through the chimney with good Saint Nick.

Up On The Housetop

TRADITIONAL
Arranged by Richard Bradley

Up On The Housetop - 1 - 1

60

Here comes Santa Claus!
Here comes Santa Claus!
Right down Santa Claus Lane!
Vixen and Blitzen and all his reindeer
Pulling on the rein.
Bells are ringing,
Children singing,
All is merry and bright.
Hang your stockings and say your pray'rs,
'Cause Santa Claus comes tonight.

Here Comes Santa Claus
(Right Down Santa Claus Lane)
By GENE AUTRY and OAKLEY HALDEMAN
Arranged by Richard Bradley

Moderately bright

Here Comes Santa Claus - 2 - 1

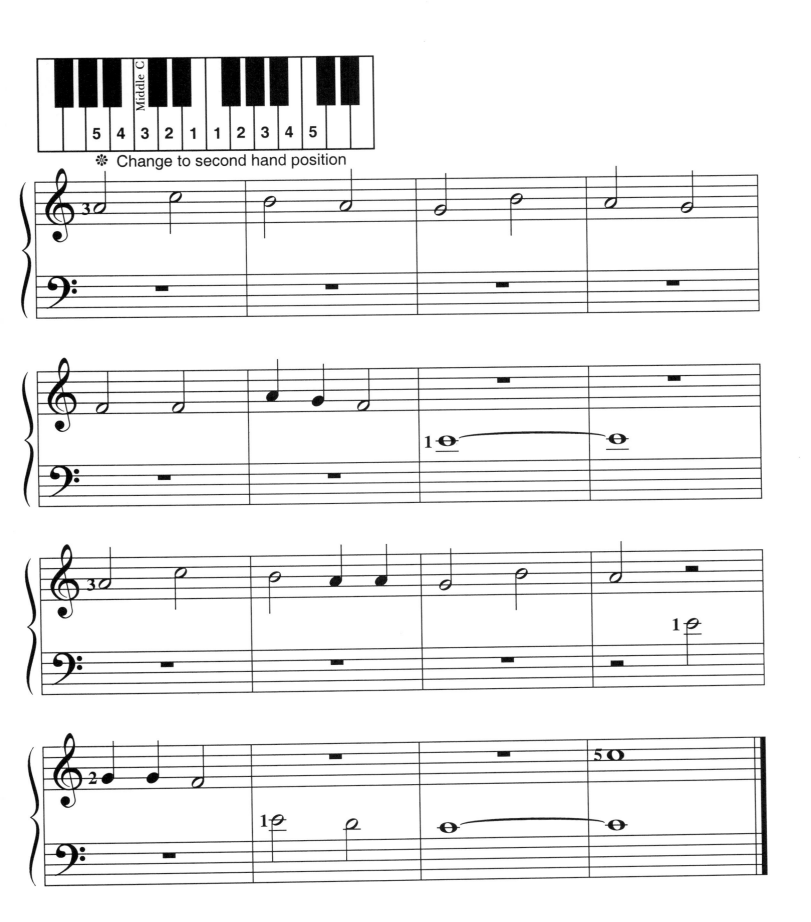

Here Comes Santa Claus - 2 - 1

Auld Lang Syne

By ROBERT BURNS
Arranged by Richard Bradley

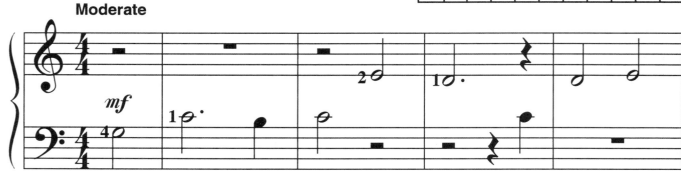

Auld Lang Syne - 2 - 1

Should auld acquaintance be forgot,
And never brought to mind?
Should auld acquaintance be forgot,
And days of auld lang syne?
For auld lang syne, my dear,
For auld lang syne.
We'll tak' a cup o' kindness yet,
For auld lang syne.

RICHARD
BRADLEY

Richard Bradley is one of the world's best-known and best-selling arrangers of piano music for print. His success can be attributed to years of experience as a teacher and his understanding of students' and players' needs. His innovative piano methods for adults (*Bradley's How to Play Piano* – Adult Books 1, 2, and 3) and kids (*Bradley for Kids* – Red, Blue, and Green Series) not only teach the instrument, but they also teach musicanship each step of the way.

Originally from the Chicago area, Richard completed his undergraduate and graduate work at the Chicago Conservatory of Music and Roosevelt University. After college, Richard became a print arranger for Hansen Publications and later became music director of Columbia Pictures Publications. In 1977, he co-founded his own publishing company, Bradley Publications, which is now exclusively distributed worldwide by Warner Bros. Publications.

Richard is equally well known for his piano workshops, clinics, and teacher training seminars. He was a panelist for the first and second Keyboard Teachers' National Video Conferences, which were attended by more than 20,000 piano teachers throughout the United States.

The home video version of his adult teaching method, *How to Play Piano With Richard Bradley*, was nominated for an American Video Award as Best Music Instruction Video, and, with sales climbing each year since its release, it has brought thousands of adults to—or back to—piano lessons. Still, Richard advises, "The video can only get an adult started and show them what they can do. As they advance, all students need direct input from an accomplished teacher."

Additional Richard Bradley videos aimed at other than the beginning pianist include *How to Play Blues Piano* and *How to Play Jazz Piano*. As a frequent television talk show guest on the subject of music education, Richard's many appearances include "Hour Magazine" with Gary Collins, "The Today Show," and "Mother's Day" with former "Good Morning America" host Joan Lunden, as well as dozens of local shows.